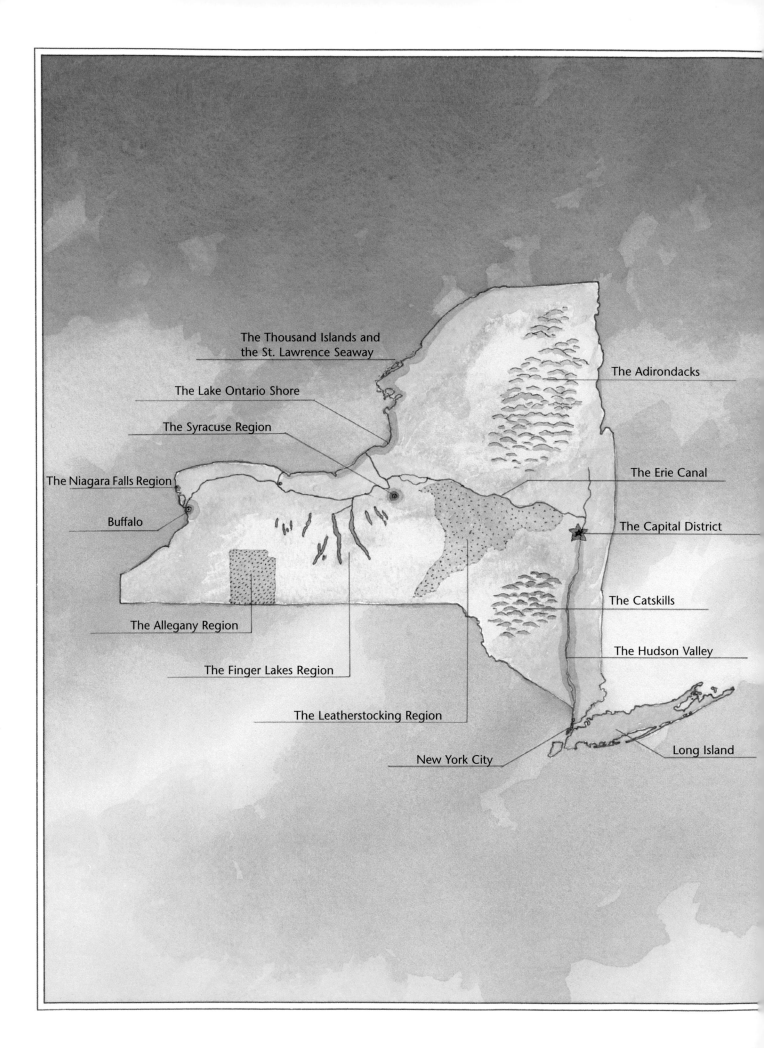

The Thousand Islands and
the St. Lawrence Seaway

The Lake Ontario Shore

The Syracuse Region

The Niagara Falls Region

Buffalo

The Adirondacks

The Erie Canal

The Capital District

The Catskills

The Hudson Valley

The Allegany Region

The Finger Lakes Region

The Leatherstocking Region

New York City

Long Island

Margery Facklam and Peggy Thomas

New York
The Empire State

Illustrated by Jon Messer

Charlesbridge

Welcome to New York, the Empire State

When you think of New York, you probably think of the Empire State Building or the Statue of Liberty. These are only a couple of the sights that millions of people come to see in New York City. But in the state of New York, you can see much more—forests and farms, towering mountains, two of the Great Lakes, thousands of smaller lakes, rivers, sandy beaches, parks, and the mighty Niagara Falls. Ancient seas and ice age glaciers carved these different landscapes. The names of many of the rivers, lakes, and landmarks remind us of the earliest people who lived there.

Peter Stuyvesant, Dutch Governor 1646–1664

Dutch trading ship circa 1620

Algonquin Natives

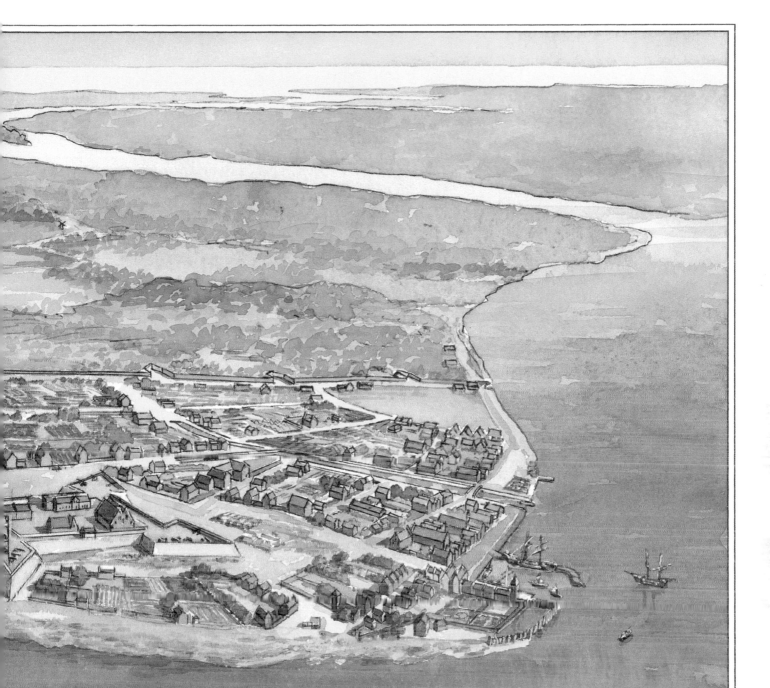

Long before Europeans arrived, many nations of Native Americans made the land of New York their home. The Algonquins lived along the coast and up the Hudson River Valley. The Seneca, Cayuga, Onondaga, Oneida, and Mohawk occupied central and western New York.

When Dutch and British settlers arrived, they built towns and forts, cut down trees, and farmed much of the land. Later the Erie Canal opened between Albany and Buffalo, making it easier for people to move west. New towns and cities grew, and so did the state.

George Washington called New York the "Empire State," and it still lives up to that name. Come see for yourself!

Central Park, which was designed by Frederick Olmsted, covers 843 acres of woodlands and grassy fields. You can walk, bike, ride horseback on the many trails, rent a boat to paddle on the lake, or ice skate here in winter.

Millions came to America through New York Harbor. They were greeted by the Statue of Liberty. A gift from France in 1886, Liberty is 305 feet tall and made of steel and copper. As they passed Liberty, immigrants were taken to Ellis Island. Between 1892 and 1954, more than twelve million people were welcomed to the United States at Ellis Island. Now you can visit the island's museum.

New York is a city of islands, which means it is also a city of bridges and tunnels. The Lincoln Tunnel and the Holland Tunnel run under the Hudson River. The Brooklyn Bridge was the first to cross the East River, and at that time it was the longest steel suspension bridge in the world.

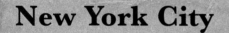

New York City

It was easy to sail ships into the large natural harbor at the mouth of the Hudson River, so that's where early settlers stayed. When Dutch traders arrived in the 1600s, they gave the Native Americans trade goods worth about twenty-four dollars in exchange for the land they called Manhattan. The Dutch named their new settlement New Amsterdam, but when the English took over, they changed the name to New York.

New York was the first capital of the new nation. But it quickly grew into a world center for business, politics, and culture. Today more than eight million people from all over the world live in New York City. It is the headquarters of the United Nations and home to both the Empire State Building and Times Square, where America ushers in the New Year.

w York City is famous for its music, art
leries, and theaters, including Radio City
usic Hall, the Metropolitan Museum of Art,
d Lincoln Center. It is also the center of
evision broadcasting and book publishing.

September 11, 2001, the twin
vers of the World Trade Center
lapsed after a terrorist attack.
ere is now a memorial on the site
those who lost their lives that day.

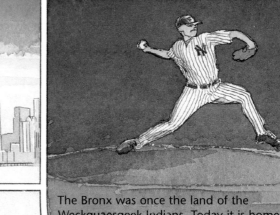

The Bronx was once the land of the
Weckquaesgeek Indians. Today it is home to
more than 600 different species of animals
at the Bronx Zoo, 250 acres of rare and
beautiful plants at the New York Botanical
Garden, and thousands of baseball
fans at Yankee Stadium.

Long Island

On a map Long Island looks like a great whale basking between Long Island Sound and the Atlantic Ocean. Stretching almost 120 miles, it is the largest island on the East Coast. Dinosaurs left their footprints in its muddy soil when it was still attached to what is now Pennsylvania. Ice age glaciers sliced it away and pushed Long Island north to where it is today.

Lighthouses shine all over Long Island. On the eastern tip of Long Island is Montauk Point Lighthouse, which George Washington had built in 1792. It still blinks its warning for sailors. Local legend says that Fire Island, a sandy piece of land just south of Long Island, got its name from pirates who lit bonfires on the beach to lure ships to their doom. But the Fire Island Lighthouse has been guiding ships to safety since 1826.

You might not think anyone would raise cattle on Long Island, but they do. Deep Hollow Ranch in Montauk is the oldest cattle ranch in the nation. Cattle have grazed on its land since 1650.

Long Island was once occupied by thirteen Algonquin tribes who thrived on the harvest from the island's rich soils and fertile fishing grounds. Today only two small groups of Algonquins remain. The Poospatuck Reservation is home to the Unkechaug Nation, and the Shinnecock Nation has a small reservation next to Southampton.

The landscape of Long Island is a patchwork of pitch pine and scrub oak forests, rich farmlands, and rolling dunes. Sandy ocean beaches stretch along the south shore, while the north shore is rockier. It is an island that has something for everyone—suburban neighborhoods, nature reserves, wealthy estates, lighthouses, fishing villages, and even cattle ranches.

The endangered piping plover is the color of sand. It is hard to see as it scurries on the beach, but its clear whistle gives it away. Its nesting sites are protected on Fire Island National Seashore.

LONG ISLAND

N

Fire Island

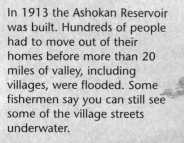

In 1913 the Ashokan Reservoir was built. Hundreds of people had to move out of their homes before more than 20 miles of valley, including villages, were flooded. Some fishermen say you can still see some of the village streets underwater.

The region is heavily forested with oak, cedar, pine, and birch, but it's the sugar maples that are tapped every spring to produce delicious maple syrup. New York is second to Vermont in maple syrup production in the United States.

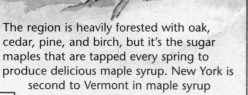

Bald eagles compete with the fishermen. They soar high above the mountains and through valleys, scanning streams for their next meal of fresh fish. Not long ago, eagles were an endangered species. Now the Catskills has one of the largest populations of bald eagles in the Northeast.

The Catskills

Only a hundred miles from New York City are the Catskill Mountains. Catskill means "wildcat creek" in the language of the original Dutch settlers. In the 1900s people took trains to huge resort hotels in the Catskills to enjoy clean water and mountain air. Today the clean mountain water is brought to New York City. Hundreds of miles of tunnels and aqueducts collect water in the mountains and send it to reservoirs that supply ninety percent of New York City's water. The water is so clean that it does not have to be specially filtered.

Flashes of silver in a fast-moving stream mean that trout are running. Each spring fishermen come to the Catskills to try their hand at fly-fishing, a sport that started in the Catskills. Fishermen make a lure called a "fly," which looks like an insect. The fly is used to coax a hungry trout to bite.

West Point is a military school built on a high cliff overlooking a bend in the river. It was at this bend that George Washington ordered his men to string a 150-ton iron chain across the river to keep British ships away. There's no chain now, but West Point is still a military academy, the oldest in the United States. If you visit West Point, be sure to see Washington's "watch chain."

Washington Irving is one of New York's most famous writers. He lived in the Hudson Valley. You can visit his home, called Sunnyside, and walk the streets of Sleepy Hollow. That name was made famous in Mr. Irving's scary story "The Legend of Sleepy Hollow," in which the main character, Ichabod Crane, was chased by the headless horseman.

The Hudson Valley

In 1609 Henry Hudson was searching for a route to Asia when he sailed the *Half Moon* up a river the Algonquin Indians called Mahicanituk, meaning "always flowing waters." He didn't discover the route to Asia, but he did find a rich inland territory along the river that would later be called the Hudson. The river is really an estuary, or bay, where tides rise and fall as far north as Albany. It is more than two hundred feet deep in some places, and the banks are steep. So it was a good place for military men to set up camp, because from there they could see enemy ships. It also became an ideal spot to build factories and mills, and a beautiful location for millionaires to build their mansions.

ne of the places everyone wants to see
 the Franklin Delano Roosevelt
ational Historic Site in Hyde Park. The
tate was Roosevelt's home, and he
ade many decisions there as our 32nd
esident. He and his wife, Eleanor
oosevelt, led America through the
reat Depression and World War II.
e was the only president voted
 to four terms in office.

Even though it was more than 50 miles from
the ocean, Hudson was a whaling town. It was
such a popular place that it came within one
vote of becoming the state's capital. Now it is
home to the country's largest collection of
firefighting equipment at the American Museum
of Firefighting.

The short-nosed sturgeon is one of New
York's most endangered fish. It lives in the
Hudson River. When toxic waste was
dumped into the river in the early 1900s,
the giant sturgeons nearly died out. Now
that people obey the clean water laws, these
ancient fish are making a comeback.

15

The Capital District

Sitting along the shore of the Hudson River is the Capital District. It was once a battleground, but now it is where New York laws are made. Area names like Voorheesville and Guilderland are reminders of the early Dutch settlers. In 1664 the British captured the Dutch city of Fort Orange and changed its name to Albany, in honor of the Duke of Albany. It became the state capital in 1797. The state's lawmakers meet in Albany to pass bills that affect all New Yorkers. They even passed the bill created by a fourth-grade class from Syracuse to adopt the apple muffin as the official state muffin.

Just outside of Albany a cliff rises 2,000 feet above the fertile farmland. Because Indians used this cliff as a way across the small mountains that stand here, some early settlers named it Indian Ladder. The Dutch called them the Helderbergs, meaning "clear mountains." Today they are a rich site for collecting fossils.

The historic city of Troy is the home of Uncle Sam. Sam Wilson was a meatpacker who stamped "U.S." on the products he shipped to the United States military. During the War of 1812, soldiers joked that his initials meant Uncle Sam, and we've been saying that ever since.

One of the state's most beautiful insects is the rare Karner blue butterfly, which lives in the sandy Pine Bush region around Albany. It feeds and lays its eggs only on a plant called the blue lupine. As more people move in, there is less space for wildlife in the Pine Bush region. Conservation efforts are helping both the lupine and the Karner blue butterfly survive.

The soothing mineral waters seeping up from Saratoga Springs and the thunder of speeding racehorses attracted rich tourists to the town of Saratoga in the 1800s. Horses still run on one of the country's oldest tracks and are celebrated in the National Museum of Racing and Hall of Fame.

The Leatherstocking Region

Legend has it that Abner Doubleday shooed cows from a pasture and invented baseball near Cooperstown. That may not be true, but today Cooperstown is the home of the National Baseball Hall of Fame. Thousands of tourists also stroll the streets of the 19th century village at the Farmer's Museum.

One of the most endangered animals in New York literally clings to life in the mist of the Chittenango waterfall. It is the tiny ovate amber snail. This is the only place in the world to find it.

On a hot summer day, it's nice to cool off in the underground caves of Howe Caverns. These caves were formed millions of years ago by rushing underground rivers. Now you can take an elevator 156 feet down into a world of towering stalagmites and dripping stalactites. You can even take a boat ride on the underground Lake of Venus.

The English settlers who roamed the Mohawk Valley in the 1700s wore leather leggings, or leatherstockings. The Leatherstocking Region then became the backdrop for many tales written by James Fenimore Cooper. Four big rivers outline the region—the Mohawk to the north, the Delaware and the Susquehanna to the south, and the Chenango to the west. The landscape is riddled with underground caverns and rich mineral deposits. These plentiful resources attracted businesses large and small, from knitting mills in Utica to the IBM computing company in Binghamton.

The Erie Canal

DeWitt Clinton was governor of New York when construction on the Erie Canal began in 1825. People called it "Clinton's Ditch," because they didn't think it could be done. But it turned out to be the longest canal in the world, built in the least time, with the least experience, for the least money. The 363-mile canal linked the Hudson River with the Great Lakes. New tools had to be invented to build eighty-three locks that would lift boats 565 feet from the Hudson River to the higher level of Lake Erie.

The canal changed the way people lived. Instead of seven weeks on horseback, they could travel across the state in only seven days on a barge pulled along a towpath by horses or mules. Cities to the west grew and prospered. Now the canal is mostly a waterway for pleasure boats, but some barges still haul heavy loads.

When the Erie Canal was opened in October 1825, there were no telegrams, phones, television, or computers. News of the opening was carried by the booming of cannons, one after another, across the state from Lake Erie to the Hudson River. It took an hour and 20 minutes to pass on the message that the canal was open.

Near the very spot where the first shovelful of earth for the Erie Canal was dug on July 4, 1817, you can still ride on a packet boat and hear "hoagies," or canal men, call to their mules. The Erie Canal Village in Rome recreates a canal town complete with craftsmen.

A great blue heron stands tall and still along the banks of the canal. Fuzzy red staghorn sumac, Queen Anne's lace, wild grapevines, and milkweed line the towpath.

At the Erie Canal Museum in Syracuse, you can climb aboard the *Montezuma*. It is a life-size copy of the first canal boat to reach Syracuse. The museum building was the last weigh lock left on the canal. Boats had to pull in here to get weighed. The heavier the load, the more money the captain paid in tolls.

The Iroquois, who call themselves Haudenosaunee, meaning "People Building a Long House," still govern themselves in one of the oldest living democracies. The center of the Iroquois Nation—Seneca, Cayuga, Onondaga, Oneida, Mohawk, and Tuscarora—is five miles south of Syracuse. Representatives of each nation meet there for the Grand Council. The Iroquois have eight reservations that help preserve their culture, traditions, and national identity.

Most people think Buffalo is the snow capital of New York State, but Syracuse gets the most snow. The average snowfall each winter is 114 inches, from squalls that sweep south from Lake Ontario. But skiers and ice fishermen don't mind a bit.

The Syracuse Region

Early settlers called Syracuse "Salt City" because it was the only place in North America to find large amounts of this "white gold," which they needed to preserve meat and cure animal hides. Native Americans and early settlers collected salty brine from the marshlands along Lake Onondaga. When they boiled the water in big kettles, salt was left. Later they learned to let the sun do the work of evaporating the water to leave the crystals of salt.

The Adirondacks

In 1892 New York State set aside six million acres of land in the Adirondack forest as "forever wild." Adirondack Park is larger than the parks of Yellowstone, Grand Canyon, and Yosemite combined. Thousands of lakes and more than thirty thousand miles of brooks, streams, and rivers flow through these ancient mountains. Each winter people come to ski the slopes of Whiteface Mountain and Gore Mountain. And each summer they fish, swim, and paddle canoes in the clear waters of Lake Champlain, Lake George, Saranac Lake, and Raquette Lake. Although it was once heavily logged, today this rugged land still has more hiking trails than roads and more trees than people.

Mount Marcy, also known as Cloudsplitter and Tahawus, is the tallest mountain in New York. It is more than a mile high. The Hudson River starts here as melting snow and runoff, then flows south to the Atlantic Ocean.

Lake Placid is the most famous Adirondack lake because two Olympic Winter Games were held there. In 1980 the American hockey team unexpectedly beat the team from the Soviet Union. It was called "the miracle on ice."

Beavers are common in the Adirondacks now, but they had almost disappeared from New York by 1909. Trappers killed beavers for their fur. Today beavers are protected by conservation laws.

Fort Ticonderoga was called "the key to the continent" when the French built it in 1755 to protect their land. But four years later, the British captured the fort. In the Revolutionary War, Ethan Allen and the Green Mountain Boys captured it for the new Americans. It's open now to the public.

The Thousand Islands and the St. Lawrence Seaway

Legend has it that the Great Spirit gave the Iroquois people the gift of a beautiful garden. But when the tribes argued, the Great Spirit picked it up and took it away. Tiny pieces of the garden fell from his hands and landed in the St. Lawrence River to make the beautiful Thousand Islands. There are actually more than eighteen hundred islands. Some are tiny juts of rock with a cottage no bigger than a playhouse. Others have large summer mansions for the very rich. Mary Island and Wellesley Island are state parks where people can dock their boats, camp, and go fishing.

Everyone travels by boat in the St. Lawrence Seaway, but they must watch out for the giant oceangoing freighters that silently cruise toward Lake Ontario or to the ocean. The United States and Canada created a channel connecting the Great Lakes to the ocean through the St. Lawrence River. When the St. Lawrence Seaway opened in 1959, ocean freighters could travel all the way to Minnesota.

Freighters carrying cloth from Scotland or cars from Japan must be lifted 42 feet in the locks at Massena in order to get to the Great Lakes. At the Dwight D. Eisenhower Lock, you can stand on the viewing platform and watch huge ships make this climb.

Campgrounds are everywhere on the islands and along the river's edge. Every spring, bass fishermen come from all over the country to try for the $10,000 prize in a contest to catch the biggest bass.

Boldt Castle on Heart Island is a home where no one ever lived. In 1895 millionaire George Boldt began building it for his wife. Workers constructed a 120-room stone castle with its own bowling alley, elevator, and playhouse. When his wife died suddenly, Mr. Boldt was so sad that he stopped construction. Now tourists can see the castle just as it was left 100 years ago.

The Lake Ontario Shore

Lake Ontario is the smallest of the Great Lakes, but it has a huge influence on the kind of weather that is perfect for fruit crops. New York State is second in the nation for raising apples, but many miles of cherry, peach, and pear orchards also thrive along Lake Ontario's shore. Rochester is the largest city on the south shore of Lake Ontario. It is the home of Eastman Kodak Company, which began with George Eastman's invention of a handheld camera that everyone could afford to buy.

The long flight across Lake Ontario is tiring for migrating birds. Many stop to rest at the Iroquois Wildlife Refuge. Here geese and ducks paddle in the water and bald eagles nest in basswood trees. Closed-circuit cameras focused on the eagles' nest give visitors a close-up view of eggs hatching and feeding time for eaglets.

The endangered Massasauga rattlesnake is found in only two swamps in this region. It is shy and rarely seen. Most of the time it stays hidden in crayfish holes or other murky places where it can find food.

The south shore of Lake Ontario was protected by several forts. Fort Niagara stands at the mouth of the Niagara River. The oldest building in this region is the fort's stately French Castle, built in 1726. In the War of 1812, a soldier's wife, Fanny Doyle, became a hero by loading cannons when the fort was under attack. Fort Oswego, just north of Syracuse, protected the eastern edge of the lake from French and British attacks.

When you walk through Genesee Country Museum in Mumford, New York, you may think you are living a hundred years ago. It's a real pioneer village with a blacksmith shop, a tavern, a schoolhouse, a bank, houses, and other buildings.

This region is famous for its grapes. Because the Finger Lakes do not freeze over in the winter, this warm, humid microclimate is perfect for growing grapes, cherries, and other fruit. California is the only state that produces more grapes for wine than New York.

Harriet Tubman is famous for her work as a nurse, scout, Union spy in the Civil War, and one of the most famous conductors on the Underground Railroad, which helped slaves escape to freedom. You can visit her home in Auburn.

More than 6,000 acres of swampland make up the Montezuma National Wildlife Refuge. Dead trees sticking up out of the murky water give it a spooky look. But it is home to more than 240 species of birds, including more than 140,000 Canada geese that migrate through the area each spring and fall.

The Finger Lakes Region

In the heart of the state, the Finger Lakes look as though God pressed his hands into wet clay. The ten lakes, lined up like fingers on two hands, were formed by forceful glaciers raking across the land at the end of the ice age thousands of years ago. The glaciers also left behind vast waterfalls, gorges, and fertile land perfect for growing grapes, apples, and other produce. The largest lakes—Canandaigua, Keuka, Seneca, Cayuga, and Owasco—got their names from the Native Americans who called this area home. Just as the Native Americans were attracted to these shores, so were early settlers, followed by pioneers in technology and social change.

The first Women's Rights Convention was held in Seneca Falls in 1848. Now the National Women's Hall of Fame celebrates the ideas and actions of women such as Elizabeth Cady Stanton, Susan B. Anthony, Amelia Bloomer, Elizabeth Blackwell, Harriet Tubman, and others who made life better for many people.

When you walk through the gates of Chautauqua Institute, the narrow streets are filled with people talking about last night's opera or a dancer they met. Music floats down to the lake from students practicing in tiny cabins and from stars performing in the open-air theater. Kids swim and learn to sail while their parents take classes or listen to lectures.

Salamanca is the only city in New York State on land owned by a Native American tribe. It is also the home of the Seneca-Iroquois National Museum. Today more than 80,000 Native Americans of many nations live in this state.

The Genesee River races through the steep gorge at Letchworth State Park and crashes over three waterfalls. The park is called the Grand Canyon of the East.

The Allegany Region

South of Buffalo, on the shore of Lake Erie, is a region that appeals to people from all walks of life. This is the home of the Seneca Indians, known as "Keepers of the Western Door," and a large Amish farming community. People also come here to enjoy art and music at the world-famous Chautauqua Institute. Chautauqua Lake is the region's finest fishing spot east of Lake Erie, especially for fishermen hoping to catch a "muskie." That's the nickname for the muskellunge, the largest fish in the lake. Allegany State Park is New York's largest state park, with miles of trails to hike and bear caves to explore.

Roger Tory Peterson wrote and illustrated hundreds of bird books. He helped protect endangered species, including the bluebird. At the Roger Tory Peterson Institute in Jamestown you can see his original paintings and walk the nature trails.

The Amish choose to live with no electricity, phones, television, or computers. Instead of cars, they trot down the street in horse-drawn buggies.

Buffalo and the Western New York Region

In the 1800s the Erie Canal emptied into Lake Erie, and Western New York became a great shipping port. Buffalo, the center of it all, was called the City of Light. In 1901 almost every building at the Pan American Exhibition blazed with light, powered by the new electricity made in Niagara Falls. There were more millionaires in Buffalo at that time than anywhere else in the United States. Now Buffalo is famous for its chicken wings, the Buffalo Bills, the Albright-Knox Art Gallery, and the Buffalo and Erie County Botanical Garden, which was built in 1898.

William McKinley was the 25th president. He was shot and killed at Buffalo's Pan American Exhibition on September 6, 1901. His vice president, Theodore Roosevelt, was hunting in the Adirondacks. When Roosevelt arrived in Buffalo, he took the oath of office at the Wilcox Mansion, which is now a museum.

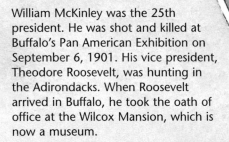

Grand Island, in the Niagara River, lies between Buffalo and Niagara Falls. It is the largest freshwater island in the world. Many years ago it was famous for the huge white oak trees that were cut and shipped to England to build sturdy clipper ships. At Beaver Island State Park, people play golf, swim, play on the beach, or fish. At Buckhorn Island State Park, they hike through the nature sanctuary.

In Buffalo's harbor you can climb aboard the WWII destroyer *USS The Sullivans,* a submarine called the *USS Croaker,* and the guided missile cruiser *USS Little Rock.*

ell-O jiggled into existence in LeRoy, New York. That is where Pearle B. Wait, a cough-yrup maker, mixed gelatin and fruit flavors. His wife, May, named it Jell-O.

Cows are a common sight all through New York State, but Western New York is prime dairy country. Milk is New York's leading agricultural product, and New York is the third-largest milk producer in the nation.

The Niagara Falls Region

Niagara Falls is the name of a city, New York State's oldest state park, and one of the most famous tourist attractions in the world: the falls of Niagara. The water rushing over the falls starts in Lake Superior and flows all the way to the Atlantic Ocean. Millions of years ago, the falls poured directly into Lake Ontario, but the pounding waters dug out the gorge to where the falls stand today. As rocks break off, the falls move back a little every day. More than one hundred fifty thousand gallons of water flow over the falls every second! But that flow would be even more powerful if not for the nearby hydroelectric power plant that diverts some of the water before it falls.

Rare gnarled cedar trees more than 500 years old grow in the Niagara gorge. The gorge is also an important winter home for more than 200 kinds of seagulls. The air is warm, and the fast-moving water supplies plenty of fish for both birds and fishermen.

The town of Lewiston was an important stop on the Underground Railroad. There, runaway slaves found help and were hidden in the cellars of several houses. At nightfall people rowed them across the Niagara River to safety in Canada.

Seventeen daredevils have gone over the falls in barrels, a jet ski, a kayak, and other odd containers. Five were killed. Others have walked or ridden a bicycle across the gorge on a tightrope. But the most amazing event was the rescue of seven-year-old Roger Woodward after his family's boat was wrecked in the rapids. He was the first person to go over the falls and survive while wearing only a life vest.

Maid of the Mist boats sail so close to the base of the falls that the passengers have to wear raincoats to keep from getting soaked in the mist. Since 1846, when the first Maid of the Mist boat was launched, there has never been an accident, but their crews have rescued people from the Niagara River.

Visitors can drive or walk across the Rainbow Bridge between Niagara Falls, New York, and Niagara Falls, Canada. The bridge is named for the beautiful rainbows that appear when the sun shines through the mist.

Conclusion

Were you surprised to discover that New York is more than tall buildings and busy streets? Each region is rich with vibrant cities and small towns, big industries and quiet farms. As one of America's oldest states, it boasts the largest city in the country, as well as the largest complex of public wild land in the eastern United States. It is home to many American symbols such as Uncle Sam, the Statue of Liberty, baseball, and even Jell-O.

But it is the people who made New York the Empire State—the Native Americans, the early settlers, and the millions of immigrants who entered this country through New York City's Ellis Island. They made their mark on New York's history. It is this great variety of people—building, inventing, exploring, preserving, and enjoying New York State—who will continue to shape its future.

Symbols of New York

State motto: The state's motto is Excelsior, a Latin word meaning, "ever upward."

EXCELSIOR

State bird: The bluebird was once a rare sight in New York State. But schools and other organizations have helped the bluebird by putting up special nest boxes.

State mammal: The beaver was adopted as the state mammal in 1975.

State fish: Trout are common in streams and lakes throughout the state.

State beverage: Each year thousands of New York cows produce millions of gallons of mi the state beverage.

State tree: The sugar maple provides New Yorkers with maple syrup as well as wood for fine furniture.

State flower: The rose was chosen as the state flower in 1955.

State fruit: The apple is the state fruit. Settlers brought the first apple seeds to New York in the 1600s.

State fossil: The scorpion-like eurypterid became extinct more than 200 million years ago. The largest fossil of one found in New York State was 10 feet long.

State insect: The ladybug, or ladybird beetle, became the official state insect in 1989. It helps farmers and gardeners by eating pesky aphids that eat plants.

State gemstone: The red garnet of New York State is used for grinding glass and polishing metal. The Barton Mine on Gore Mountain is the world's largest source of garnets.

Resources

To learn more about New York's wildlife and history, check out these books:

Harness, Cheryl. *The Amazing Impossible Erie Canal*. New York: Simon and Schuster Books, 1995.

Knight, Frank. *New York Wildlife Viewing Guide*. Helena, MT: Falcon Publishing, 1998.

Ogintz, Eileen. *The Kid's Guide to New York City*. Old Saybrook, CT: Globe Pequot, 2004.

Stewart, Mark. *All Around New York: Regions and Resources*. Chicago: Heinemann Library, 2003.

Stewart, Mark. *New York History*. Chicago: Heinemann Library, 2003.

Stewart, Mark. *New York Plants and Animals*. Chicago: Heinemann Library, 2003.

Stewart, Mark. *Uniquely New York*. Chicago: Heinemann Library, 2003.

Try these and other websites for more information about New York State. (Please note that addresses can change.)

NYS Department of State Kid's Room
http://www.dos.state.ny.us/kidsroom/menupg.html
Read about the history of the state, discover important places to visit, and learn facts about the state seal and symbols.

I Love New York
http://www.iloveny.com
Have fun with puzzles, games, state facts, and even online postcards.

New York Wild
http://www.newyorkwild.org
Check out this site about New York wildlife. It features recorded images from webcams focused on the nests of bald eagles, ospreys, great horned owls, and other New York State animals.

New York State Department of Environmental Conservation
http://www.dec.state.ny.us
Find information about some of New York's endangered animals and what is being done to protect them.

To my children, Thomas, David, John, Paul, and especially Peggy, my co-author—M. F.

For Katie, Dan, and Francis—P. T.

For Melissa and Kristen—the sunlight on my face, the sparkle in my eye—J. M.

Text copyright © 2007 by Margery Facklam and Peggy Thomas
Illustrations copyright © 2007 by Jon Messer

Published by Charlesbridge
85 Main Street
Watertown, MA 02472
(617) 926-0329
www.charlesbridge.com

Library of Congress Cataloging-in-Publication Data
Facklam, Margery.
    New York: the Empire State / Margery Facklam and Peggy Thomas ; illustrated by Jon Messer.
        p. cm.
    ISBN 978-1-57091-660-1 (reinforced for library use)
    ISBN 978-1-57091-661-8 (softcover)
1. New York (State)—Juvenile literature. I. Thomas, Peggy. II. Messer, Jon. III. Title.
F119.3.F33 2007
974.7'1—dc22   2006009025

Printed in China
(hc) 10 9 8 7 6 5 4 3 2 1
(sc) 10 9 8 7 6 5 4 3 2 1

Illustrations done in watercolor on Arches paper
Text type set in Monotype Baskerville; display type set in Knockout
Color separations by Chroma Graphics, Singapore
Printed and bound by Jade Productions
Production supervision by Brian G. Walker
Designed by Susan Mallory Sherman